A SPIRIT DAUGHTER WORKBOOK

WRITTEN BY
JILL WINTERSTEEN

FOR THE FULL MOON
WEDNESDAY, APRIL 5TH, 2023
9:34PM PT

LIBRA FULL MOON

In the midst of Aries Season, in between two New Moons in Aries, we have the Full Moon in Libra, bringing some Air to our Fire. While Aries Season asks us to focus on ourselves and the soul's mission, Libra reminds us that we live in a world with other people. These people also have a soul's mission and purpose. In order for everyone to feel that their mission is honored, supported, and respected, there needs to be compromise, conscious listening, and the willingness to let go. This Moon is a time to survey our relationships and decide if they are limiting or supporting us. It's a time to feel how we can encourage others to find their life's journey and decide how to walk our individual paths together.

Ruled by Venus, the planet of love and beauty, Libra reminds us to connect with what we love in life. Libra also helps us connect with our hearts and communicate with others from this place. In its highest energy, Libra gives us patience, compassion, and the willingness to understand other people's perspectives. Living with others is not always easy, but when we do it through the lens of love, it becomes less challenging. Staying within the higher vibration of love is not always possible; we are affected by many things within and around us, including the people we interact with each day. We naturally absorb other people's energy, especially when we have an intimate relationship with them. We take on other people's energy, emotions, and even thoughts. We become like the people we are around because energy is contagious.

On this Full Moon, it's important to have some boundaries around your heart, mind, and energy. These boundaries aren't meant to be harsh to others. They are meant to protect your peace. Libra helps us understand the impact of our relationships on the soul's mission. First, though, this energy helps us understand how to create peace within ourselves. Boundaries help create and maintain inner harmony. When we allow others to affect our energy, emotions, and thoughts, we lose control over our peace. We stop defining the vibration we live in and instead absorb from others the vibrations around us.

A lack of boundaries can look like many things. It may be saying yes when we really mean no. It may look like people-pleasing or being afraid of upsetting someone. It may also look like oversharing emotional issues with people who aren't supportive, or feeling like you are a dumping ground for other people's emotions. A lack of boundaries can make you feel a bit annoyed almost all of the time, and you may get angry easily. Anger is often a sign that your boundaries are being invaded. You may be angry at another for crossing them or angry at yourself for not upholding them. As you move through this Full Moon, become aware if you need more boundaries between yourself and others. Another clue that more boundaries are needed is if you easily take on other people's energy. For instance, you may be in a pleasant mood. Then, after an encounter with someone in a lower vibration who is complaining a lot, you find yourself in a lower frequency too. Boundaries help us hold the vibration we want to experience instead of taking on someone else's.

LIBRA FULL MOON

Creating strong boundaries is part of being in healthy relationships. When we maintain our boundaries, we can align with the soul's mission more easily. We can also prioritize our needs while still showing up for other people. We don't feel drained or annoyed by others. Instead, we give what we can when we can. When both people in a relationship do this, they can have clear, conscious communication around expectations and compromises. Boundaries also help us. They create a bubble around our peace and help us center ourselves. When we don't have healthy boundaries, the world pulls at our energy from different directions. Our emotions feel unstable, our thoughts are scattered, and we find it hard to focus. When we have firm boundaries in place, we can focus clearly on what's important and limit our distractions in life. This focus helps us clarify and stay aligned with the soul's mission.

Boundaries, though, require balance. We need just enough to protect our energy but not so many we keep away people who add to our lives. This is why healthy boundaries in relationships are so important. We want people in our world. We want to share our existence with others. It feels good to connect with other people. Some of the most joyous moments we have are spent with others. We also naturally crave people to share our stories, sorrows, and success. We also crave love and people to love. Love is the highest vibration of all. It helps us touch our souls. Yes, we can love ourselves, but love for others also helps expand our hearts and raise our vibration. We want people in our lives, and we even need them. But we also need boundaries so relationships don't become limiting or draining. We need balance, and creating that balance is what this Full Moon is all about.

This Full Moon is an opportunity to assess all of your relationships and boundaries within them. As you move through this Full Moon, feel centered in yourself. Know that you are whole without anyone. Then begin to look at the connections in your life. Which ones nourish you? Which ones drain you? Where do you need more balance? Where do you need more boundaries? Relationships also change over time. What was once working well for both of you may need some repair.

When looking at your relationships, it's important to remember your life's mission. Align with the Sun in Aries this Full Moon to feel your soul. What does it want and need from others? Look at how your relationships are supporting your life's mission. Notice places where you may compromise what you need for the sake of other people's happiness. Also, look to see how you are supporting another's life mission. Ideally, in relationships, two people are able to co-exist and share a life together while staying aligned with their individual life paths. This co-existence can be challenging, as both parties have needs and priorities. When working in a relationship, decide what you absolutely cannot negotiate on, or you will feel you are betraying yourself. Then decide where you can compromise and loosen some boundaries. Then look to the relationships that can support these decisions and the ones that cannot. If any relationship feels contrastive or unsupportive this Full Moon, now is the time to readjust it or release it.

When releasing relationships, it's important to honor them and what they taught you. Some relationships aren't meant to continue forever. Some occur because two people have karma, and once that karma is worked out, the relationship fades. As you sit with the light of the Moon, decide what relationships are ready for release and what you need in order to let them go. Then align with the Full Moon, say goodbye to them, and create space for new connections ready to continue you forward on your soul's path.

LIBRA MOON X ARIES SUN

Every Sun Season has its opposing Full Moon. For Aries, the sign of the Self, that Full Moon is in Libra. Aries Season inspires us to align with our purpose and make following it our highest priority. Aries asks us to be bold and decisive, and to take action quickly based on instinct alone. Aries reminds us that we have the power to overcome any obstacle or challenge along our way. We are our greatest asset and never need to rely on anyone or anything else because we are all we'll ever need. On the other hand, Libra teaches us that while our life's mission is of great importance, our inner peace is the highest priority. Nothing is as important as maintaining inner harmony. Furthermore, when we are energetically settled, we see clearly. Our path is drawn out in front of us, and we know the next steps to take on it. We also know what to do in the face of adversity. A true warrior is calmest in the midst of battle. Libra helps us cultivate inner peace and use it as our greatest tool during times of challenge.

Libra also teaches us that our path is that much sweeter when shared with another. The challenge, though, is staying true to our own journey while supporting another on their unique path. When in a partnership of any kind, it becomes easy to drift from our path onto theirs, and vice versa. It takes a deep awareness from both people to not only stay true to their individual purposes but to nurture each other's life mission. It becomes easier if both people involved have processed their life's mission and can articulate it in a way that the other understands. As with everything in life, though, there are trade-offs. To be in a fully committed relationship, compromises are often needed for the partnership to thrive. Our job becomes knowing what is negotiable in our world and what is off the table. We need to pick our battles, knowing when to fight and when to go with the flow. When we do dig in our heels, it needs to be from a place of harmony and gratitude for one another, not from an emotional reaction.

To truly master the art of relationships, we need to understand both Aries's and Libra's low vibrations. When we become aware of these frequencies within ourselves, we can shift and release them. Once free of these shadows, we can fully integrate Libra's and Aries's highest vibrations to form relationships that support each other in a beautiful co-creation of each other's life journey and purpose. We learn to develop healthy relationships in which each person maintains their sense of identity. Furthermore, we can respect each other's boundaries and admire them for their gifts, raising their vibration each day from a place of completeness within ourselves. To achieve a high-vibrational relationship, we start by searching for and shifting the lower vibrations, which undermine our energetic unions.

Libra has two main shadow sides: indecision and passive aggressiveness. Libra views the world as parts of the same whole, all equal. This view, although beautiful, can lead to indecision because all choices are equal. Indecision can lead to anxiety because we inherently know that time is limited, and when we fail to make choices, we delay our life and its journey. This anxiety eats away at our inner peace, disturbs our well-being, and muddles any relationship until we choose to begin and move forward again. At its lowest point, indecision can cause us to follow someone else's choice only to find out later we are unhappy and need to realign ourselves with our path. Some relationships can survive this readjustment, while others break under the pressure and the redirection of energy.

Libra's other low side of passive aggressiveness causes us to become manipulative as we try to control a situation without clearly stating our needs. When we align with this side of Libra, we may become stubborn, procrastinate, or even avoid people. We play games and cause drama where it is unneeded simply because we are afraid to express our true feelings. In some cases, the relationship does not hold space for us to share our emotions. These types of relationships need to be adjusted so that we feel safe expressing ourselves, or they need to be released. In other cases, we may have never learned how to clearly state our needs and felt that our only option was manipulation to acquire the energy we needed to feel supported in the world. If this is the case, finding awareness and compassion is the first step to understanding how these patterns were formed. We need to honestly look at how we gain support or energy from others through passive tendencies. To shift these behaviors, we need to become comfortable asking for what we need. Communication is key in any relationship. The more we can speak our truth firmly, but without aggression, the better off our partnership will be.

It may not happen overnight, but each of us can learn how to express our needs in a nonpassive approach and receive the energy we deserve from another. Likewise, we can learn how to give energy to the relationship so the other person feels their needs are met and their dreams are nurtured. It's important, though, to understand that our main source of energy comes from ourselves and the connection we have with the Universe. The energy we gain from another is never meant to sustain us or deplete them, or vice versa. In a truly high-vibrational relationship, each person is abundant with energy and gives freely while also receiving frequencies from another. It is a beautiful cycle of reciprocity in which both people are connected to themselves, their purpose, and each other.

On this Full Moon, we also need to look at Aries's low sides of selfishness and aggressiveness. Aries's lower vibrations cause us to act without thinking, relying on pure instinct alone, even if it means not including others in our decisions. The lowest side of Aries is pure selfishness. When we align with this side, we forget we live in a world full of other people. We put our needs first at the expense of others, and we forget the importance of empathy. We see the world only through our eyes and resist understanding it through someone else's perspective. We bulldoze our partners, not hearing what they have to say, and leave them feeling unheard and not respected. We become like a bull in a china shop, causing emotional havoc everywhere we roam.

Aries's other low vibration is aggressiveness with controlling behavior. When we align with this side, we become demanding, bossy, and overly assertive. We intimidate others by yelling or asserting our power in a dominating way. This low side of Aries comes from our own internal conflict. When we align with these vibrations, we are at war with ourselves. We project this aggression onto others and start unnecessary battles. We seek to win to make ourselves feel better, but what we really need is to resolve our internal issues, triggers, and pain before engaging with another. We need to ask ourselves what the anger is a reaction to. What is the underlying emotion? And what needs to be healed?

If we look at the spectrum of energy involved in this Full Moon, on one end, we have aggression and control. On the other end, we have passivity and indecision. None are beneficial in the realm of relationships. Think over your actions in partnerships. Do you recognize any of these patterns in yourself? Know that it's ok if you do. You always have the opportunity to shift these vibrations. Have compassion for yourself first, and know that this Full Moon's work is to bring these shadows to light. Find the root of these behaviors and shift them into the higher vibrations each sign brings us. The most challenging step of any change is awareness. Align with the Moon to see yourself fully and know that you are capable of shifting any energy within you. As you begin to vibrate higher, you'll create and attract higher-frequency relationships that elevate your soul's journey.

ASPECTS

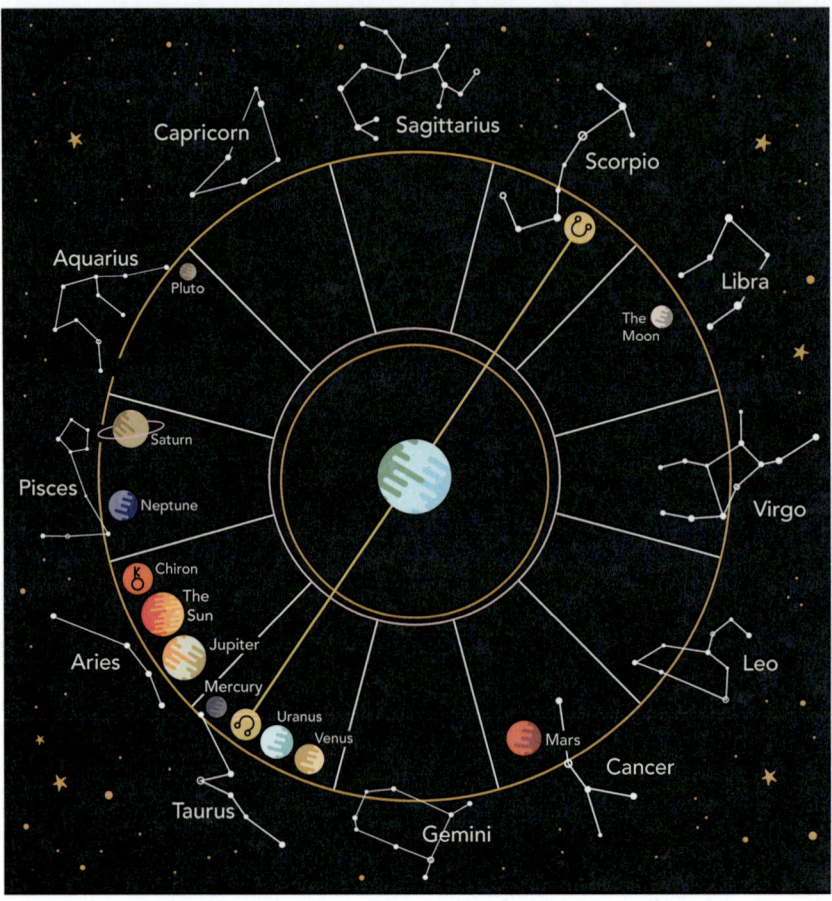

We have a few aspects to work with this Full Moon other than the opposition between the Sun and Moon. The Sun is conjunct, or next to, Chiron and Jupiter, while the Moon opposes these cosmic bodies. Chiron is classified as a comet and a minor planet. It orbits the Sun between Saturn and Uranus. In astrology, Chiron is known as the wounded warrior. This energy represents the transformation of painful experiences into life wisdom. Chiron teaches us how to confront and accept our past. Through this acceptance, we can turn our past pain into our personal power. If we cannot completely heal our own wounds, we can gain the wisdom to help others with theirs.

Chiron's energy on this Full Moon helps us understand how our past affects our present. This especially applies to our relationships. Throughout this Full Moon, feel how your past experiences in partnerships may be affecting your present ones. When we go through painful or traumatic experiences, it can be challenging to leave them in the past. We can feel that they are happening in the present moment as the mind cannot separate yesterday from today. We may even find ourselves projecting our past pain onto others or assuming a traumatic experience will occur again.

ASPECTS

As you review your relationships, look for patterns that may reveal misplaced energy. Do you, for instance, attract the same type of relationship over and over? Or do you place expectations on current relationships based on past ones? It's also important to look at boundaries in the context of your past. Traumatic events, especially in childhood, can impact our ability to form healthy boundaries in present-day relationships. Notice if you people-please or say yes when you mean no because you are afraid of a past pain resurfacing. Perhaps you fear, that if you create boundaries, a current partner will treat you like someone in the past who hurt you. Notice if you are giving more than you are receiving because of an old pattern of fear. Anytime you fear creating a boundary will cause you to lose love or acceptance, it is an indication that an old pain may be at the root of your fear.

As you work with Chiron this Full Moon, remember that you may not be able to change your past, but you can make sure it does not affect the way you show up for yourself or others.

Jupiter's involvement in this Full Moon challenges us to expand past our fears and step into our highest versions of ourselves. Jupiter is the planet of expansion and compels us to dream big and assume the best will happen. Jupiter is quite a different energy compared to Chiron, making this Full Moon feel dynamic with energy. Jupiter in Aries encourages us to find our potential and never sell ourselves short. This energy wants us to feel the immensity of the soul and align with it. It wants us to believe in ourselves and our purpose. It also wants us to take huge leaps of faith that will manifest the life we are meant to live.

As this energy opposes the Full Moon, we are compelled to look at how our relationships may be limiting our expansion. Relationships, like all things, can become a comfort zone. You may stay attached to certain people, places, or things because they feel comfortable. This doesn't always mean they are good for your evolution or your soul. Over this Full Moon, notice if you are holding on to any relationship out of comfort or fear of the unknown. This may include relationships with people, projects, locations, or even knowledge. You can tell a relationship that is out of comfort because you stop growing while in it. You feel that you are simply going through the motions day in and day out with no change. This may manifest as relationships that keep you small or distract you from your potential. It may also look like unsupportive relationships that do not hold space for you to change. It may also manifest as relationships that cycle through the same set of dramas over and over with no resolution or learning.

As you look at your relationships this Full Moon, keep in mind Jupiter's energy. Are your relationships expansive? Do they make you feel abundant in love, time, and support? Or are they draining or distracting? Relationships that don't match your potential may need to be readjusted or released this Full Moon. If someone doesn't believe in you, they may not be the right fit for your life. Jupiter teaches us to focus on partners who can support our potential and even help us walk the path of finding it. Commit to creating those relationships this Full Moon, starting with the relationship with yourself. Remind yourself of how worthy you are of your potential, and believe in the immensity of your soul.

RELATIONSHIP SCOPES

Your Sun sign is the astrological sign the Sun was in when you were born. It is the topic of most horoscopes you see in magazines and so forth. You also have a Moon sign, which tells you the sign where the Moon was located in the sky when you were born. You can look up yours at astro-charts.com. Your Moon governs your emotional body and tells you what your heart is here to learn in this lifetime. Look to your Moon to understand why you call certain people into your life, how you love, and what you need in a relationship.

Your Moon sign also describes your reigning needs. These are the energies that make you feel fulfilled and aligned with your life. When you feel happy, content, depressed, or angry, it is often because you are either addressing or ignoring your Moon's needs. You must meet your own emotional needs before you can be in a harmonious relationship with others. Furthermore, you ideally want partners who understand, sympathize with, and support your needs while understanding their own. This harmony occurs more easily between certain Moon signs compared to others.

Below is a brief explanation about your Moon's needs from yourself and in a relationship. There are also compatibility suggestions. Know that any Moon sign can get along with any other Moon sign as long as both embody their higher potential. Every energy has a low, or shadow, side and a high side. Embodying this high side will be easiest with your Most Compatible signs. Your Opposites Attract Moon sign is the most reflective in pointing out what lower sides you are embodying and can help you release them. These relationships can be frustrating but very illuminating. Your Growth Edge Moon signs are very different in their expression of emotions but will help you evolve and understand your subconscious on a deeper level. They are different from you but offer a perspective that is easy to digest and understand. The last category, Greatest Challenge, are signs that you may find challenging to maintain a high vibration with. This difficulty doesn't mean it's not possible. It's just challenging. It takes a lot of shadow and trigger work for these relationships to succeed, but if both parties are up for the challenge, these relationships can help you evolve to new, undiscovered places.

RELATIONSHIP SCOPES

ARIES MOON:
Your reigning need is adventure. You are on a mission to go bravely where no one has gone before and call in situations that help you develop the courage to climb the tallest mountains. You are fiercely independent and seek the freedom to follow your heart at any cost. In relationships, you need someone who has the same passion for life and shares your love of adventure. You require time alone to pursue challenges on your own. It is best for you to have self-assured partners who give you the freedom to roam while pursuing their own passions. Your biggest trigger in a relationship is indecisiveness. You need someone who knows what they want, even if it differs from what you want. Confidence is key, and you'd rather debate with someone than help them vacillate between ideas. A high-vibrational relationship for you consists of two people who take turns allowing the other to lead and are always up for new adventures that spice things up.

Most Compatible Moon Signs: Aries, Leo, Sagittarius
Opposites Attract: Libra (be aware of their indecisiveness)
Growth Edge: Gemini, Aquarius
Greatest Challenge: Cancer, Capricorn

TAURUS MOON
Your reigning need is peace. Your heart craves steadiness in your inner and outer worlds. When flustered, your emotions are soothed by nature, and you need to incorporate Mother Earth into every area of your life. You also need to connect with your sensory emotions to feel the world around you, including other people. You mainly rely on the language of touch to express your feelings. In relationships, you need someone who understands your need for stability and respects your comfort zones, helping you stay within them until you are ready for the unknown. If you feel rushed, you dig in your heels and can act like a stubborn child. You feel most comfortable with people who understand your need for peace. Drama and games are not your things. They only leave you feeling insecure and frustrated. You are honest and forthright, and you need someone who can meet you eye to eye in the present moment. Once you find your match, though, you commit for the long haul and even tend to stay long past the relationship's expiration date. A high-vibrational relationship for you consists of two people who make each other feel secure and are comfortable getting lost in the moment together.

Most Compatible Moon Signs: Taurus, Virgo, Capricorn
Opposites Attract: Scorpio (be aware of their need to psychoanalyze)
Growth Edge: Cancer, Pisces
Greatest Challenge: Leo, Aquarius

GEMINI MOON
Your reigning need is to have your emotions understood. You are on a mission to express your feelings and share them with the world. Sometimes, though, you share too much before you know what it is you feel. You do best with partners who can help you sit with your feelings and understand them. Your love language is speech, and you need someone willing to have in-depth conversations with you and truly listen to your words. In relationships, you do best with people who nourish your natural curiosity about the world and enjoy exploring it with you. Steer clear of people who feel threatened or annoyed by your urge to talk to everyone you come across. You may come off a bit flirtatious, but that is not your intent. Seek a partner who is secure in themselves and encourages you to interact

with those around you—and most importantly, who trusts you. A high-vibrational relationship for you consists of two people who trust each other and are willing to talk through challenges with open minds.

Most Compatible Moon Signs: Gemini, Libra, Aquarius
Opposites Attract: Sagittarius (be aware of their overwhelming visions)
Growth Edge: Leo, Aries
Greatest Challenge: Virgo, Pisces

CANCER MOON

Your reigning need is to feel your heart. You, more than any of the Moon signs, need to feel. You need nourishment, and you need quiet contemplation. You also need to feel your intuition and honor it. When aligned with your intuition, you can leave the confines of your shell and be vulnerable to others. You can receive and give energy from a place of contentment. You work best with partners who respect your need to feel and are willing to ride the waves of emotions with you. It is also important that they acknowledge the inherent power of your emotions. When you have the space to feel, you instinctively make the best decisions for yourself and anyone around you. When you don't feel appreciated or your gifts are not reciprocated, you retreat behind your fortress. You crave a connection that allows you to tear down your walls and people who appreciate the beauty held within them. A high-vibrational relationship for you consists of two people willing to give and receive emotionally when needed.

Most Compatible Moon Signs: Cancer, Scorpio, Pisces
Opposites Attract: Capricorn (be aware of their determined nature)
Growth Edge: Virgo, Taurus
Greatest Challenge: Libra, Aries

LEO MOON

Your reigning need is self-expression of the heart. You need to sing your song and roar your roar. Furthermore, you require a partner who supports your expression and uses gentle encouragement to help you develop it. You are here to understand your worth and learn to take up space with your presence. Once you realize that you are a true gift to everyone you meet, you will finally feel free to be yourself. In relationships, you need the freedom to express yourself, whether it be dancing around the kitchen or professing your love through generous acts of service. You need playfulness in your life and partners who can communicate this way. Steer away from people who belittle you or make you feel self-conscious. Your partner needs to make you feel like the queen or king you are. They need to be grateful to stand in your presence. Their reward for this admiration is your loyal heart, which is big enough to heal the world. A high-vibrational relationship for you consists of two people who cheer each other on and have mutual admiration for each other's gifts.

Most Compatible Moon Signs: Leo, Sagittarius, Aries
Opposites Attract: Aquarius (be aware they don't compete for the same audience)
Growth Edge: Libra, Gemini
Greatest Challenge: Scorpio, Taurus

VIRGO MOON

Your reigning need is service. You rely on logic, organization, and your skill set to navigate through life. You also rely on these things to understand your emotions, but logic and emotions often don't mix. Your mission is to feel your intuition over your practical side and lean into it as your guide. Doing this will help prevent overanalysis and deep self-criticism, which you are prone to feeling. In relationships, you thrive when you are of service. You love to do things for others and need people who appreciate you. You also do best with partners who are organized and know where they are headed in life. While you can hold space for people to figure out their game plan, your patience quickly runs out when there is too much fluctuation. You also do well with partners who acknowledge your emotions and help you process them. In order to express yourself, you need to feel comfortable and not under judgment, which can be challenging for a perfectionist. At your deepest level, you are trying to heal and heal others. If you remember this and have compassion for yourself, it will help all of your relationships. A high-vibrational relationship for you consists of two people who appreciate each other and are willing to share praise for each other's gifts.

Most Compatible Moon Signs: Virgo, Capricorn, Taurus
Opposites Attract: Pisces (be aware not to interpret them as indecisive)
Growth Edge: Scorpio, Taurus
Greatest Challenge: Sagittarius, Gemini

LIBRA MOON

Your reigning need is inner harmony. Your heart needs to find peace within first, then find relationships that support this peace. You also require equality and respect. To form a high-vibrational relationship, your partners must treat you as an equal, as you do them. You tend to suppress your emotions through indecision. In relationships, you do best with people who bring out your true desires and inspire you to follow your heart—even if your mind is wavering. You also do well with partners who speak the language of touch, which helps you leave your head and connect with your body, the source of your inner knowing. You can debate any subject and do well with people who challenge you while respecting your opinion. Steer away from partners who belittle you or make you feel that your opinion isn't of value. Also, stay away from those who do not understand your love of beautiful things. You take pleasure in your surroundings and enjoy co-creating an environment that is energetically and aesthetically pleasing. Find someone who wants to find the perfect shade of paint with you and understands that this process is a form of meditation for your soul. A high-vibrational relationship for you consists of two people who make balance and peace a priority, working to create it in all aspects of their lives.

Most Compatible Moon Signs: Libra, Aquarius, Gemini
Opposites Attract: Aries (be aware of their assertiveness)
Growth Edge: Sagittarius, Leo
Greatest Challenge: Cancer, Capricorn

SCORPIO MOON

Your reigning need is intimate understanding. Your emotions run deep, and you like it that way. You're on a quest to understand the depths of your own subconscious. Before any external relationship can exist, you must first form a deep bond and trust with yourself. You need to understand your inner workings, and then maybe you'll share them with another. Any relationship with you is full of intensity. When you find your match, you tend to bond for life. You love to feel you are alone in the world with your partner and are quick to create a sanctuary where you both can reveal your innermost secrets. You do not allow just anyone into your cave, though. Your walls are high, and you require a partner who respects them. Anyone who tries to bulldoze down your borders before you are ready will quickly feel the sting of the Scorpio. Trust is important to you, and it takes some time for anyone to earn it. If you feel your trust has been broken, you become suspicious of every action and even paranoid. If your suspicions are proven right, it's best to move on. You have a tough time recovering from betrayal. When in a healthy relationship, though, you can step into your full power and steer the ship for both of you from your deep, intuitive knowing. A high-vibrational relationship for you consists of two people who are willing to look at their shadows and grow together as they unravel them.

Most Compatible Moon Signs: Scorpio, Pisces, Cancer
Opposites Attract: Taurus (be aware of their fear of the unknown)
Growth Edge: Virgo, Capricorn
Greatest Challenge: Leo, Aquarius

SAGITTARIUS MOON

Your reigning need is truth. You need the freedom to roam wherever your heart desires. You know there is more to life than what is right in front of you, and you crave the bigger picture. You also need optimism in your life, both from yourself and others. In relationships, you bring the energy of excitement and are often the one who inspires spontaneous road trips and unplanned outings. You have a natural faith that everything will work out and require partners who have that same trust in life. You do well with people who understand your quest for adventure and can keep up with your wanderlust. When in a relationship, you attract signs and serendipity for both of you. Any partner needs to acknowledge this gift and appreciate you for it. They also need to appreciate your stunning sense of humor and ability to light up any room. Steer away from people who feel inhibited by your brilliance and resentful of the attention you often attract. A high-vibrational relationship for you consists of two people who respect each other's freedom and know how to have a good time together.

Most Compatible Moon Signs: Sagittarius, Aries, Leo
Opposites Attract: Gemini (be aware of their logical side)
Growth Edge: Libra, Aquarius
Greatest Challenge: Virgo, Pisces

CAPRICORN MOON

Your reigning need is security. Your emotions run deep, although very few people are privy to them. You tend to conceal your feelings and need a safe space to express them. You also need space and solitude to understand yourself before you can trust another. In that space, you find your intuition, which guides you to your life's work. Of all the Moon signs, your career plays the largest role in your emotions. To feel fulfilled, you must find work that makes you feel useful, needed, and of service. You need a purpose, and you require partners who understand this need. In relationships, you often take charge, as you know what you want and when you want it. You secretly would love to relax and allow someone else to call the shots, though, as long as they call them correctly. Work on being attracted to partners who are consistent and able to commit fully to your heart. You do not have the patience for people who flake on plans or act differently in various situations. A high-vibrational relationship for you consists of two people with steady hearts and clear visions for themselves and each other.

RELATIONSHIP SCOPES

Most Compatible Moon Signs: Capricorn, Virgo, Taurus
Opposites Attract: Cancer (be aware of their emotional side)
Growth Edge: Scorpio, Pisces
Greatest Challenge: Libra, Aries

AQUARIUS MOON

Your reigning need is freedom. You are on a mission to find your most authentic self, and you stop at nothing to accomplish this purpose. You like to experiment with different methods of living and loving that do not conform to any societal norms. You crave the chance to apply your eccentric ways to change the world, and you need a purpose that fulfills your heart. You need space to be yourself and partners who respect this need. In relationships, you defy convention. You do not allow society to define you in any way, and relationships are no different. You require partners who understand your need to dance to your own rhythm and who support each step. You express yourself through speaking and often engage in lengthy discussions about the ways of the world. You do best with someone who can keep up with your quick-witted intelligence and sense of humor. Steer away from people who are clingy or emotionally needy. You often react to these energies with aloofness and detachment, undermining the relationship. A high-vibrational relationship for you consists of two people who stand in their truth, are willing to express it, and always have reverence for each other—even when they disagree.

Most Compatible Moon Signs: Aquarius, Libra, Gemini
Opposites Attract: Leo (be aware of their need for approval)
Growth Edge: Sagittarius, Aries
Greatest Challenge: Scorpio, Taurus

PISCES MOON

Your reigning need is expansion of the heart. You are on a mission to become one with the Universe. Give yourself time and space for deep contemplation and meditation to explore the depths of your emotional body and nourish your creativity. You feel everything, including the emotions of those around you. It's important to take time to decipher which feelings are yours and which ones are another's. You do not need to block out others' feelings; you just need to understand their source and understand how to release them. You require partners who understand that you are a highly emotional being who operates from a place of feeling over logic. Your intuition is strong, and with the right partner, it is nourished. You also do best with partners who support and encourage your imagination. You crave creative outlets that allow your expansive visions to bloom and are vehicles for your healing. When you have a partner who can meet you on a soul level, you can dive even deeper into your consciousness. If you feel you are not met at the soul level, you may become aloof and even resort to methods of escapism to hide from your feelings. A high-vibrational relationship for you is two people willing to bare their souls and explore the deepest emotions without fear.

Most Compatible Moon Signs: Pisces, Cancer, Scorpio
Opposites Attract: Virgo (be aware of their structured ways)
Growth Edge: Capricorn, Taurus
Greatest Challenge: Sagittarius, Gemini

---

*You can look up your personal Moon Sign at astro-charts.com

VENUS PLACEMENTS

Libra's planetary ruler is Venus, making this planet's energy active on this Full Moon. One of the ways of understanding how this Full Moon will affect you is to look at your Venus placement. Just as we all have Sun and Moon signs, we also have a Venus sign. This is the zodiac constellation that Venus landed in when you were born. You can look up your Venus placement at astro-charts.com. As Libra meets the Full Moon, your Venus placement will become energized and motivated. You will feel these vibrations in more depth today than on other days. Below is a description of your Venus placement and how it will be affected by this Full Moon.

VENUS PLACEMENTS

VENUS IN ARIES: You are here to love fiercely and with courage. You desire strong intimate connections full of fire and passion. You need to surround yourself with people who will honor your intensity and meet you at the level you want to be seen. You may, at times, overwhelm others with your passion and love for life. It's important for you find partners who can accept your overabundance of love and give back to you in return. On this Full Moon, feel your fire and decide which partnerships deserve it. It's also important for you to have firm, healthy boundaries. If you feel your heart or energy is being invaded, you align with your warrior side, and sparks fly. If you notice yourself getting annoyed or frustrated in a relationship, it may be a clue that you need stronger boundaries.

VENUS IN TAURUS: You desire peace and serenity in your love life. You have no patience for drama or emotional roller coasters. You need to surround yourself with people who value ease and comfort just as much as you do. You also enjoy a deep connection with and love of nature. Your relationship with Mother Earth is just as important as your other relationships. Make sure to nurture it throughout your life. On this Full Moon, survey your partnerships and decide which ones bring you peace and which ones disturb it. Become aware of why you allow people in your life who do not honor your need for calm. Is there something you are trying to heal by connecting with these people? As you focus on boundaries this Full Moon, make sure you have enough of them in place to protect your inner sanctuary. Not everyone deserves access to your energy.

VENUS IN GEMINI: You are here to communicate the language of love. You have a strong desire to talk to your partners and listen to what they have to say. You need to surround yourself with people who are willing to open up to you and have deep conversations. You have no patience for people who play games or have walls around their hearts. You want to hear your partner's deepest desires, and you want them to be open to yours. On this Full Moon, decide which partners are giving you the energy you need and which ones are frustrating or draining you. You have a lot to offer a relationship. You inspire new adventures and can bring energy to any encounter. It's important for you to ensure you are getting equal energy in return. Many people will be happy to receive your vibrant vibration, but only some will be able to fill you up in return.

VENUS IN CANCER: You love deeply and need partners who can love deeply in return. You desire strong bonds with people that will last a lifetime. You crave routine and the familiar. You find beauty in knowing where you'll wake up each day and with whom. Your home and family are central to what makes you feel good about life. It's also what helps you devote time to self-care. When you feel stable at home, you are able to show up for yourself on all levels. On this Full Moon, review your relationships and decide which ones feel supportive and which ones don't. Also, notice if you are asking for what you need and then allowing yourself to receive it. Part of your journey this lifetime is to learn to receive love from others. Because of this, you may find yourself in partnerships that drain you and do not give back to your heart. If any of these relationships are in your life, take the opportunity of this Full Moon to adjust or release them.

♀ FIND THIS SYMBOL IN YOUR CHART TO FIND WHAT SIGN VENUS IS IN.

VENUS PLACEMENTS

VENUS IN LEO: You love loudly and fiercely. You desire partners who can celebrate life and your very existence with you. You want to be cherished, and you want to cherish someone else. You want deep heart connections where both parties prioritize the relationship. You need to surround yourself with people who are expressive in their hearts. You have no patience for closed-off people or those who cannot simply say, "I love you." On this Full Moon, decide which connections are serving your heart and which ones feel like a mental drain. Not everyone's partnership will have the energy you crave. You have a natural exuberance for life. Find people who match it. You connect with others from your heart. If your partners cannot meet this connection, it may be time to look for ones that can.

VENUS IN VIRGO: You are practical and grounded in your heart. You desire partners who share the same groundedness. You have no patience for games or manipulations. You want someone who can view you as their equal. You do not want to be the grown-up in the relationship. You need to surround yourself with people who value life's purpose and genuinely want to give back to the collective. On this Full Moon, review your relationships and decide which ones feel like an equal exchange of energy. This is also a good time to feel your boundaries in relationships. You desire a structured life full of joy and abundance. You need partners who respect your need for routine and understand that daily practices create a container for happiness. Protect your peace by protecting your routines and allow only people who respect your need for these things to enter your life.

VENUS IN LIBRA: You possess natural charm and charisma, which attracts many partners. You desire ones who respect your need for peace and inner calm. You need to surround yourself with people who can remain unruffled even when in the midst of chaos. You have a naturally calm demeanor and need partners who have the same love of inner harmony. You have no patience for drama or overexaggerated emotions. On this Full Moon, review your relationships and decide which ones are bringing drama to your world. Are any of your relationships disturbing your peace? Or are they protecting it? Align with Libra and your Venus Placement on this Full Moon to bring equanimity and balance to your partnerships. Tips the scales so that each person feels supported, seen, and heard. Release any energy that feels draining, manipulative, or codependent.

VENUS IN SCORPIO: You have a natural love for the truth. You crave a deep understanding of love, life, and the Universe. You dive deep when it comes to love. You desire deep connections and the type of intimacy only a few can meet. You never settle though. You will not meet someone on a superficial level. It's either the depths of the ocean or nothing at all. You also crave partners who are willing to explore complex psychological topics with you. You want to know someone through and through. If they are not willing to open up and dive in, then you prefer to walk alone. On this Full Moon, decide which relationships are deserving of your intensity and which ones cannot meet it. You have no problem spending time with yourself. Release any relationships that cannot give you the intense connection you crave, and be content with being with yourself until the right match for your energy comes along.

VENUS PLACEMENTS

VENUS IN SAGITTARIUS: You love freedom and find beauty in the open road. You need partners who understand your desire for knowledge and understanding. You are in love with life itself. You crave to see and understand all the world has to offer. You will stop at nothing to come into contact with new experiences that expand your heart. On this Full Moon, feel what types of partnerships will nurture your love of adventure. How do you maintain freedom when committed to another? Partners who can begin to answer this question deserve a place in your life. Also, recognize that your relationships extend to places and locations. Where do you need to travel next to fulfill your heart? Decide which relationships need tending to have them flourish into a new existence.

VENUS IN CAPRICORN: You have a natural love of order and structure. Disciplines, practices, and routines make your heart happy. You want your heart to be taken seriously by others and yourself. You make deep commitments with your energy and will connect only with others who can do the same. You crave rootedness and stability in your partners. If someone is not willing to show up as their true self, you'd rather spend time alone. On this Full Moon, decide which partnerships are meeting you at the level you crave. You are not superficial when it comes to love. Honor your need for serious commitments and release any relationship that cannot give you what you deserve. Spend some time alone this Full Moon, as that's when your heart opens the most. Listen to it and give it space to feel.

VENUS IN AQUARIUS: You do not conform to the normal definitions of love. You have your own set of rules for relationships. Some people will understand them, some won't. You need to surround yourself with people who respect your radical self-expression and even encourage it. Your heart is enormous, and you have a lot to give. What you give, though, is unexpected. On this Full Moon, decide which relationships nurture your uniqueness and which ones question it. It's ok if not everyone agrees with you, but it's important that your partners support your need to be yourself. If a relationship feels constrictive or like it's holding you back from being yourself, it may be time to release it.

VENUS IN PISCES: You have a natural love of spirituality and all that it entails. Your relationship with your spiritual practice is important to you and is at the heart of all of your other relationships. The more connected you are with your universal consciousness, the more deeply you connect with others. You need to surround yourself with people who understand your mystic nature and are willing to support it. On this Full Moon, feel where you need more boundaries in your life and relationships. You are naturally very empathic, making you open to taking on others' emotions and insecurities. While you can be of service to others through this empathic nature, you also need boundaries to protect your peace. Become aware if any of your relationships are taking advantage of your caring nature and taking too much from your brilliant light. Know that setting boundaries does not disconnect you from others. They allow you to connect more deeply with yourself.

* *Learn more about your planetary placements with our Natal Chart Video Series at spiritdaughter.com*

LIBRA LUNAR FLOW

SUN SALUTATION A // 3 ROUNDS

Stand at the top of your mat. Inhale, stretch your arms overhead > Exhale, fold forward > Inhale, lengthen out your back > Exhale, step back to Plank Pose and lower to the ground > Inhale, reach your chest up for Cobra Pose, legs on the ground > Exhale to Downward-Facing Dog Pose. Stay here for 5 breaths and feel your entire body expand. On exhale, step to the top of the mat > Inhale, lengthen through your spine > Exhale, fold forward > Inhale, come up to standing, reaching arms overhead > Exhale, hands to your heart. Pause for a moment and feel yourself centered throughout your body.

FORWARD FOLD WITH TWIST

Step your feet hips' distance apart > Exhale, fold forward over your legs, lowering hands to the ground > Inhale, lengthen out through your spine > Exhale, lift your left arm to the ceiling, twisting to the left, and slightly bend your right knee if needed or place a block under your right hand. Stay in this twist for 5 breaths before switching sides.

CRESCENT POSE WITH TWIST

From a Forward Fold, step your right foot back into a lunge > Inhale, lift your torso and bend into your front (left) knee, raising your arms to the sky. Take 5 breaths here > Exhale, twist to the left, reaching your right arm forward, left arm back. Keep your hips facing the front of the mat and breathe deeply for 5 breaths > Exhale, place your right hand down about a foot away from your left foot, and reach your left arm to the ceiling. Take 5 more breaths here, lengthening your spine on each inhale and twisting more on each exhale. Release your left hand down and step forward into a Forward Fold and repeat on the opposite side. Once you return to the top of your mat, inhale as you rise to stand.

WARRIOR 1> PYRAMID POSE > TWISTED TRIANGLE

Stand at the top of your mat. Inhale, lift your arms > Exhale into Chair Pose > Inhale > Exhale, fold forward > Inhale, lengthen through your spine > Exhale, Plank Pose into Chaturanga (elbows bent) > Inhale into Upward-Facing Dog (chest lifts, hands and tops of the feet stay on the ground) > Exhale, Downward-Facing Dog > Inhale, step your left foot forward for Warrior 1, back foot remains flat and turning in at a 60° angle. Bend into your front knee and lift your arms. Remain here for 5 breaths, lengthening your torso. On exhale, lower your arms to the ground and hop your back foot in 12 inches toward your front foot > Inhale, lengthen your spine as you straighten your front leg > Exhale, fold over your front leg. If your hamstrings are tight, use blocks under your hands. Breathe here for 5 breaths, lengthen through your spine on each inhale, and fold deeper on each exhale. Inhale, lengthen, and place your right hand on a block inside your left foot > Exhale, rotate your spine to the left, lifting your left arm to the sky. Keep your hips level and feel just your spine rotating. Take 5 breaths here, twisting a little more on each exhale. Release both hands to the ground, stepping back into Plank Pose on exhale and lowering into Chaturanga > Inhale, Upward-Facing Dog > Exhale, Downward-Facing Dog. Repeat on the right side, ending back at Downward-Facing Dog.

CHAIR POSE > CHAIR POSE TWIST

Return to the front of your mat. Keep your feet together and bend deeply into your knees as if you were sitting in a chair. Reach your arms upward to the sky and look up. Feel your belly drawing in, helping direct your tailbone to the floor. Bring your hands to heart center, palms pressing > Exhale,

LIBRA LUNAR FLOW

twist to the left, and hook your right elbow on the outside of your left knee for leverage. Hips stay square as you twist deeper on each exhale. Feel your two sides integrating as you twist across your spine. Take 5 breaths in the twist, then return to center. Fold forward over your legs for 1 breath. Return to Chair Pose and repeat the twist on the right side for 5 breaths, then fold forward once again. Allow your spine and neck to fully release in this fold, holding it for 5 breaths. You may grab hold of opposite elbows and bend your knees slightly if needed. Once you are finished, place your hands on your hips and inhale to standing.

LOCUST POSE VARIATION - 3 ROUNDS

From the top of the mat, inhale, reach your arms overhead > Exhale, fold forward > Inhale, lengthen out your back > Exhale, step back into Plank Pose, and lower to the ground. Lie down on your mat on your belly. Have your legs hips' width apart and press into them to create stability in your lower body. Draw your belly in and feel your abs activate to support your spine. Clasp your hands behind your back, opening your chest > Inhale, lift your chest upward into a slight backbend, reaching your arms behind you. Feel as though you are creating traction through your spine as you reach your heart forward > Exhale, lift your legs, keeping them active. Reach your feet and arms back as you expand your chest forward. Take 5 expansive breaths into the back of your heart as you open your spine. Rest in between rounds for 1 breath, then complete the pose 2 more times. Slowly return to Downward-Facing Dog.

CAMEL POSE - 3 ROUNDS

From Downward-Facing Dog, come up to kneeling with your legs hips' width apart. Press down into your shins and activate your abs. Place your hands on your hips with fingertips going up the back, if possible. Imagine your pelvis pressing against a wall and keep it there as you inhale to lengthen your spine upward > Exhale slightly, bend back into Camel. Be gentle with your back and watch your breath. Make it smooth as you deepen the backbend on every exhale. If comfortable for you, release your head back, opening your neck. Spend about 5 breaths here, then come upright slowly. Pause for a moment, then repeat, going deeper the second round.

SPINAL TWIST

Come back down to lying on your back. Hug your left knee into your chest and send it over the right side for a spinal twist. Reach your left arm out to the side, stretching through your chest. Take 5 breaths here, then switch sides. On each inhale, feel your back lengthen. On each exhale, twist a little deeper.

SAVASANA

Stretch both your legs out long on the mat and place your palms facing upward in a receptive motion. Feel your entire body supported by the ground beneath you. Let your breath become natural and feel the energy circulating through you from your practice. Place your full attention on the breath moving in and out through your nose. Allow your mind to be still and your body to be calm.

* Visit spiritdaughter.com/collections/zodiac-yoga to flow with our Libra Zodiac Yoga video.

FULL MOON MEDITATION

The following meditation can be done by yourself to enhance your relationship with yourself or with partners. Partners can include your romantic partners, close friends, coworkers, or anyone with whom you wish to improve communication.

EYE-GAZING MEDITATION - 3 MINUTES

With Yourself: Stand in front of the mirror and look yourself in the eyes. Breathe deeply as you maintain the connection with yourself. Notice what emotions come up to the surface as you stare into your own eyes. Allow these emotions to express through tears, laughter, or any other sensation. Also, notice any urges to look away or any difficulties you feel when connecting with yourself. Where do they come from? What are you having trouble accepting or acknowledging about yourself? As you look at yourself with an open, honest heart, tell yourself energetically that you accept all aspects of yourself.

FULL MOON MEDITATION

With a Partner: Begin seated in front of one another in a comfortable position. Relax your eyes, but keep them open and look directly into your partner's eyes. This contact may feel uncomfortable at first, but try to breathe through any feelings that may arise. Remember to stay present with your partner. Breathe in sync, matching your inhales and exhales. Continue to breathe together for the entire time. Relax through your shoulders and your neck as you gaze into your partner's eyes. Feel a sense of love and compassion as you look at them and know they feel this for you. If the urge to giggle comes up, allow it, but remain fully present with the energy of the person in front of you.

APPRECIATION

With Yourself: Practicing gratitude is an amazing way to raise your vibration and your relationship with yourself. Take out a piece of paper or use the pages in the back of this book to write down what qualities you are grateful for in yourself. Thank yourself for the things you do for yourself and tell yourself what you appreciate most about your own being.

With a Partner: Gratitude is essential in any relationship. We often take the people closest to us for granted because they are always there. It can be easy to fall into a routine and forget how much we appreciate the other person. For this practice, have a pen and paper handy. Write down "I am grateful for," then list three things you appreciate about your partner. Have them do the same on their paper. On your same piece of paper, write down "I feel appreciated when" and list three things your partner does to make you feel appreciated. Once you are finished, switch papers. Take turns reading your answers out loud. For the first part, say to your partner, "You are grateful for" and repeat their list. For the second part, say, "You feel appreciated when" and repeat their answers. Then have them read your list. As you each read the other's list, listen with full presence and an open heart. Be genuinely curious about learning more about your partner.

METTA MEDITATION

With Yourself: Metta is the energy of loving kindness. When we send Metta to ourselves and others, we open our hearts and raise our vibrations. Sending Metta to all beings helps strengthen your relationship with yourself and everyone you know. Breathe into your heart, feeling your chest expand and contract on inhale and exhale. Think of someone you love; this can be anyone, including a pet. Feel the love you have in your heart and see them in their happiest state. As you hold this vision of them, say, "May you be happy, may you be healthy, may you be free." Now direct your attention back to yourself and feel your heart expanding. Imagine yourself in your happiest state and say to yourself, "May I be happy, may I be healthy, may I be free." Repeat this for as many people as you can think of in your life.

With a Partner: Conclude your time together through a practice of Metta meditation. Close your eyes and imagine your partner in their happiest state. See them smiling and full of radiant light. Say to yourself, "May this person be happy, may they be free, may they be at ease." After a few moments of sending loving kindness to one another, slowly open your eyes, seeing your partner fully. Thank each other for showing up to do this work together and acknowledge the bond between you.

CIRCLE SET UP

Libra is the sign of the artist, and she inspires aesthetically pleasing environments both internally and externally. Libra reminds us that our space determines how we feel internally and vice versa. If you aspire to feel calm within, then create a space that feels calm and includes elements that align energetically with the vibration of harmony and peace. Also, choose somewhere that not only includes elements of beauty but is also free of distractions. This may be a quiet location outdoors or a space in your home that feels protected and grounded. Ideally, you want to feel at peace in your space and safe to explore the energies of the Full Moon.

Once you have your space, spend some time setting it up for your practice and Full Moon ritual. Remember, the most important piece of this Full Moon is that everything feel good to you and your energy. Include all the elements in your circle but choose colors that are soothing and inspire inner harmony. To represent Air, the element that governs Libra, include auric sprays of rose water and tuberose, diffusers filled with lavender and chamomile, or dried herb bundles created from juniper and lavender.

CIRCLE SET UP

For the Fire element, include candles scented with rose, jasmine, or geranium. You can also choose ones filled with lavender or any other scent that brings you peace and harmony. For the Earth element, include crystals that align with both Libra and Aries. For Libra incorporate Watermelon Tourmaline, Lapis Lazuli, and Lepidolite; for Aries include Carnelian, Quartz, and Desert Jasper. Place the crystals around your space intuitively, allowing the energy of the crystal to lead you. You can also create a crystal grid in the center of the circle to move the energy for the night. For Air signs, like Libra, create a spiral crystal grid with a large sphere in the middle. You can also include flowers for the Earth element and even incorporate them into your crystal grid. Roses of any kind align with the energy of Libra and can support the space with their scent and energy. Lastly, for the Water element, include a small silver bowl holding some water. You can place this bowl outside after your circle on the Full Moon to charge it overnight and create your Moon Water. Cover this water and save it for your next Full Moon circle.

WATERMELON TOURMALINE   LAPIS LAZULI   LEPIDOLITE

CARNELIAN   QUARTZ   DESERT JASPER

Once your space is set up, cleanse it with a dried herb of your choice. Cleanse in a clockwise direction, beginning at the easterly point, moving to the south, west, north, then back to the east. Imagine a white light encasing the circle, protecting it from any external energies. Before your guests enter, cleanse each one of them, then cleanse yourself. Once you have all entered the circle, pause for a moment to let the energy settle before you begin.

Follow your intuitive guidance when leading a circle. You can practice alone or in the company of others. As a guide, begin with each member introducing themselves. Talk about the astrological energy of the day and how it is affecting each one of you. Share and learn from each other about your unique experiences with this Full Moon. Give plenty of space for each person to speak. Follow your conversation with the partner work section of this book. You can then begin exploring the rest of the practices. Do them alone, but share as much, or as little, with the rest of the group as you are comfortable with. Go over the questions and continue to learn from each other's perspectives.

Once you've finished the practices, spend some time in meditation again to allow the work to integrate into your energy. Afterward, draw some cards to help tap into your intuitive guidance. The following pages include information on card pulling and reading. Close the circle by giving gratitude to everyone who chose to honor the Full Moon with you. You can even practice writing gratitude statements on a card then passing that card to the person next to you to carry home with them. Give thanks to the elements for supporting you, to the space for existing, and to the energy of the Universe for guiding you along the way.

spend time with people
who connect you to the
best version of yourself.

- spirit daughter

LIBRA PRACTICES

Relationships are fluid. They move, shift, and change just like the people in them. They require awareness and the willingness to maintain them through time. Without them, though, life would be less colorful and rich. Relationships are a fundamental part of the human experience and are something we all crave in our lives on some level. They may take work, but the right ones are always worth it.

Relationships come in all shapes and sizes. We bond with people at different times in our lives, and some people come into our world for a short time to teach us something or work out some karma. Others come into our lives for an extended period and become pivotal in our growth and evolution. An important understanding about relationships is that some are meant to last forever, while others are not. Releasing a relationship that is no longer suited for our journey can be a painful and even heartbreaking event. Letting go of certain people at the right time is often needed, though, so we can move forward. Conversely, we must also recognize the relationships worth fighting for and doing the work to make them last. It can be challenging to know where to put your energy or where to back away, but your soul will always know the answer.

On this Libra Full Moon, feel into your closest relationships. Know they are all part of your soul's journey in some way, but begin to understand them at a deeper level. Feel into the ones that have taught you something important about yourself or completed a cycle of karma. Recognize that feeling of completion with some relationships and encourage yourself to thank them and release them. Then feel into the ones that are part of the long road of your soul. Decide which relationships are worth the work to maintain them because they make you a better person. Some people in our lives inspire us to vibrate higher. They don't demand it or even ask for it, but their presence alone makes us want to reach for our higher potential. These relationships support our life's mission and even help us find it.

This Full Moon is not about looking for people who complete you. You are whole already. Your first step to developing healthy relationships is to feel complete within yourself. Every relationship you have is an extension of the one you have with yourself. Once you accept, love, and know yourself, you can understand which relationships support you in being more you. You can easily see which relationships come in for a reason or a brief moment in time and which ones are meant to be lifelong bonds. It starts, though, with feeling complete within yourself.

Know, though, that you do not need to be completely perfect, or healed, or without faults to be in a healthy relationship. Many relationships, both temporary and longer-term, bring us healing and growth. They help us change and move away from lower vibrations. The key, though, is to keep showing up for ourselves. While we may never be perfect, we do not want to make it someone else's job to heal us. They may support us in our healing journey and hold space for us to evolve, but it is always our work to unravel our shadows. A genuinely supportive partner will not rush our growth or demand it. They will sit with us on our most challenging days and allow us to feel. They will also celebrate our most incredible days and be genuinely happy for our accomplishments. To develop these relationships, we must accept who we are, wounds and all, and share ourselves willingly with the right people. We must love ourselves and, from that love, attract people who will honor and uphold it.

The following practices can help you develop a higher vibrational relationship with yourself and others. You can practice them on the Full Moon and the week after. Take your time with the questions and allow the answers to arise naturally. Know that relationship work is a lifetime journey. You can revisit these questions any time the Moon is in Libra to watch yourself grow and evolve.

LIBRA PRACTICES

1. Are there any relationships in your life you need to release? What have they taught you? What karma may have been worked out? And how can you have gratitude for them but still move on?

_____

_____

_____

_____

_____

_____

_____

_____

_____

_____

2. What does a healthy relationship feel/look like to you?

_____

_____

_____

_____

_____

_____

_____

_____

_____

_____

_____

LIBRA PRACTICES

3. What are things you need to accept about yourself to form higher
vibrational relationships? Are there areas that need healing? Or shadows
that need light? Or pain that needs acceptance?

_____

_____

_____

_____

_____

_____

_____

_____

_____

_____

4. What are some signs that you are emotionally triggered? How can you
calm yourself down before you react from old patterns?

_____

_____

_____

_____

_____

_____

_____

_____

_____

_____

LIBRA PRACTICES

5. What helps ground you in the present moment when in communication with another? How can you keep your past out of the present and respond only to what is being discussed?

_____

_____

_____

_____

_____

_____

_____

_____

_____

_____

_____

_____

_____

_____

_____

_____

_____

_____

_____

_____

_____

LIBRA PRACTICES

6. Libra teaches us that opposites can exist simultaneously. How can you accept and embrace different opinions from your partner, knowing that sometimes both of you are right? How can you see their perspective more clearly without changing your own?

_____

_____

_____

_____

_____

_____

_____

_____

_____

_____

_____

_____

_____

_____

_____

_____

_____

_____

_____

_____

_____

LIBRA PRACTICES

7. What helps you admit what you want in a relationship? What are your priorities in bringing someone else into your life?

_____

_____

_____

_____

_____

_____

_____

_____

_____

_____

_____

_____

_____

_____

_____

_____

_____

_____

_____

_____

_____

_____

_____

_____

LIBRA PRACTICES

8. What helps you set and uphold clear boundaries with people? Do boundaries come easily, or are they challenging for you? What are some things that are non-negotiable even if it feels uncomfortable to state them?

_____

_____

_____

_____

_____

_____

_____

_____

_____

_____

_____

_____

_____

_____

_____

_____

_____

_____

_____

_____

_____

_____

_____

_____

_____

LIBRA PRACTICES

9. Are you comfortable asking for support when you need it? Are you comfortable receiving it when given? Conversely, do you easily provide support when needed? Remember, support doesn't just include when times are tough. Supporting each other's happiness is also pivotal.

LIBRA PRACTICES

10. How easily can you express how you feel? What helps you understand
    your feelings more deeply? What helps you communicate them?

_____

_____

_____

_____

_____

_____

_____

_____

_____

_____

_____

_____

_____

_____

_____

_____

_____

_____

_____

_____

_____

_____

AFFIRMATIONS

Write down attributes or qualities of people in your life, or in the world, that exemplify calmness and inner peace to you. These can be whole sentences describing the person or short phrases.

_____

_____

_____

_____

_____

_____

_____

_____

_____

_____

Write down 3-5 affirmations containing pieces of the phrases you wrote about. Begin each one with "I am" and include some of the qualities you listed. Embody these affirmations each day by repeating them when you feel your inner balance become disturbed.

_____

_____

_____

_____

_____

_____

_____

_____

_____

_____

_____